Mathematical and Scientific Development in Early Childhood

A Workshop Summary

Alix Beatty, Rapporteur

Mathematical Sciences Education Board
Board on Science Education
Center for Education
Division of Behavioral and Social Sciences and Education

NATIONAL RESEARCH COUNCIL
OF THE NATIONAL ACADEMIES

THE NATIONAL ACADEMIES PRESS
Washington, D.C.
www.nap.edu

THE NATIONAL ACADEMIES PRESS 500 Fifth Street, N.W. Washington, DC 20001

NOTICE: The project that is the subject of this report was approved by the Governing Board of the National Research Council, whose members are drawn from the councils of the National Academy of Sciences, the National Academy of Engineering, and the Institute of Medicine. The members of the committee responsible for the report were chosen for their special competences and with regard for appropriate balance.

This study was supported by Contract No. ESI-0102582 between the National Academy of Sciences and the National Science Foundation. Any opinions, findings, conclusions, or recommendations expressed in this publication are those of the author(s) and do not necessarily reflect the views of the organizations or agencies that provided support for the project.

International Standard Book Number 0-309-09503-4 (Book)
International Standard Book Number 0-309-54682-6 (PDF)

Additional copies of this report are available from National Academies Press, 500 Fifth Street, N.W., Lockbox 285, Washington, DC 20055; (800) 624-6242 or (202) 334-3313 (in the Washington metropolitan area); Internet, http://www.nap.edu

Printed in the United States of America.

Suggested citation: National Research Council. (2005). *Mathematical and Scientific Development in Early Childhood: A Workshop Summary*. Alix Beatty, Rapporteur. Mathematical Sciences Education Board, Board on Science Education, Center for Education. Division of Behavioral and Social Sciences and Education. Washington, DC: The National Academies Press.

THE NATIONAL ACADEMIES

Advisers to the Nation on Science, Engineering, and Medicine

The **National Academy of Sciences** is a private, nonprofit, self-perpetuating society of distinguished scholars engaged in scientific and engineering research, dedicated to the furtherance of science and technology and to their use for the general welfare. Upon the authority of the charter granted to it by the Congress in 1863, the Academy has a mandate that requires it to advise the federal government on scientific and technical matters. Dr. Bruce M. Alberts is president of the National Academy of Sciences.

The **National Academy of Engineering** was established in 1964, under the charter of the National Academy of Sciences, as a parallel organization of outstanding engineers. It is autonomous in its administration and in the selection of its members, sharing with the National Academy of Sciences the responsibility for advising the federal government. The National Academy of Engineering also sponsors engineering programs aimed at meeting national needs, encourages education and research, and recognizes the superior achievements of engineers. Dr. Wm. A. Wulf is president of the National Academy of Engineering.

The **Institute of Medicine** was established in 1970 by the National Academy of Sciences to secure the services of eminent members of appropriate professions in the examination of policy matters pertaining to the health of the public. The Institute acts under the responsibility given to the National Academy of Sciences by its congressional charter to be an adviser to the federal government and, upon its own initiative, to identify issues of medical care, research, and education. Dr. Harvey V. Fineberg is president of the Institute of Medicine.

The **National Research Council** was organized by the National Academy of Sciences in 1916 to associate the broad community of science and technology with the Academy's purposes of furthering knowledge and advising the federal government. Functioning in accordance with general policies determined by the Academy, the Council has become the principal operating agency of both the National Academy of Sciences and the National Academy of Engineering in providing services to the government, the public, and the scientific and engineering communities. The Council is administered jointly by both Academies and the Institute of Medicine. Dr. Bruce M. Alberts and Dr. Wm. A. Wulf are chair and vice chair, respectively, of the National Research Council.

www.national-academies.org

PLANNING COMMITTEE FOR THE WORKSHOP ON MATHEMATICAL AND SCIENTIFIC DEVELOPMENT IN EARLY CHILDHOOD

CATHERINE E. SNOW *(Chair)*, Graduate School of Education, Harvard University
BARBARA T. BOWMAN, Erikson Institute, Chicago, IL
DOUGLAS H. CLEMENTS, Graduate School of Education, University at Buffalo, State University of New York
JAN DE LANGE, Freudenthal Institute, Utrecht University, The Netherlands
SHARON LYNN KAGAN, Teachers College, Columbia University, NY
KATHLEEN E. METZ, Graduate School of Education, University of California, Berkeley

VICKI STOHL, *Research Associate*
HEIDI SCHWEINGRUBER, *Program Officer*
MARY ANN KASPER, *Senior Program Assistant*

BOARD ON SCIENCE EDUCATION

Acknowledgments

As the workshop summarized in this volume demonstrated, the research base about learning in early childhood is expanding and has great potential to contribute to a broader set of national policy goals focused on making sure that all children enter kindergarten ready to learn. With this important research base in mind, the National Research Council's Center for Education (CFE) convened a workshop to focus on early learning in mathematics and science. Thanks go first to the National Science Foundation (NSF); through its grant to the Center for Education, NSF makes possible such convening events that focus on the intersections between research, policy, and practice. Examining the findings of research and their application to mathematics and science curricula for preschoolers seemed a rich and timely topic to explore. Particular thanks go to NSF's Janice Earle who facilitates the intellectual exchanges between CFE and NSF that lie at the heart of the grant and its convening events.

I thank all the expert presenters, who not only agreed to present their work, but who also participated as discussants throughout the day (see the appendices for the workshop agenda and list of participants). In CFE, both the Board on Science Education (formerly the Committee on Science Education K-12 and the Committee on Undergraduate Science Education) and the Mathematical Sciences Education Board helped to shape this event. I would also thank the members of the planning committee, who generously contributed their time and intellectual efforts to this project. Special thanks go to Catherine E. Snow who graciously agreed to chair the planning committee and offered her usual skills of leadership, both logistical and intellectual.

Thanks go to Vicki Stohl, who worked to organize and plan the workshop, Carole Lacampagne for her help in the planning stages, and to Mary Ann Kasper, who ably provided administrative assistance throughout. Thanks need to go to Heidi Schweingruber for her role in conceptualizing this workshop. Jean Moon, director of the Board on Science Education, provided her skillful and competent leadership to the project. Alix Beatty expertly wrote this report, summarizing a wide-ranging and stimulating discussion. Finally, I thank Jean Moon, Heidi Schweingruber, and Catherine E. Snow, for writing post-workshop pieces about the implications of the event for the future.

This workshop summary has been reviewed in draft form by individuals chosen for their diverse perspectives and technical expertise, in accordance with procedures approved by the Report Review Committee of the National Research Council. The purpose of this independent review is to provide candid and critical comments that will assist the institution in making its published report as sound as possible and to ensure that the report meets institutional standards for objectivity, evidence, and responsiveness to the charge. The review comments and draft manuscript remain confidential to protect the integrity of the process. We thank the following individuals for their review of this report: John A. Dossey, Department of Mathematics (emeritus), Illinois State University; Leona Schauble, Teaching and Learning Department, Vanderbilt University; Prentice Starkey, School of Education, University of California, Berkeley; Louisa B. Tarullo, Mathematica Policy Research, Inc., Washington, DC.

Although the reviewers listed above provided many constructive comments and suggestions, they were not asked to endorse the content of the report nor did they see the final draft of the report before its release. The review of this report was overseen by Milton Goldberg, Distinguished Senior Fellow, Education Commission of the States, Washington, DC. Appointed by the National Research Council, he was responsible for making certain that an independent examination of this report was carried out in accordance with institutional procedures and that all review comments were carefully considered. Responsibility for the final content of this report rests entirely with the authors and the institution.

Martin Orland, *Director*,
Center for Education

Contents

1

Introduction

BACKGROUND

Three recent reports of the National Academies address different aspects of education for very young children from a variety of perspectives. *From Neurons to Neighborhoods: The Science of Early Childhood Development* (National Research Council and Institute of Medicine, 2000) provides a detailed look at the many factors that influence development in very young children. *Eager To Learn: Educating Our Preschoolers* (National Research Council, 2001b) describes the current status of the programs in which young children are educated, setting that description in the context of recent contributions from the field of cognitive science. *Adding It Up: Helping Children Learn Mathematics* (National Research Council, 2001a) closely examines mathematics learning and describes each of its facets; although this report does not focus on the learning of very young children, its conclusions and recommendations have important implications for preschool education.

Each of these reports contributes to an evolving base of evidence that the early learning programs to which children are exposed are extremely important. Because of this research, expectations for early learning are very different than they were even as recently as a decade ago. With increased recognition of the intellectual capacities of young children (3- and 4-year-olds), as well as a growing understanding of how these capacities develop and can be fostered, has come a growing recognition that early childhood education, in both formal and informal settings, may not be helping all children maximize their cognitive capacities.

The National Research Council (NRC), through the Center for Education (CFE), wishes to build on the work in early childhood it has already done. In particular, the NRC wishes to focus on research on young children and their learning of mathematical and scientific ideas. The workshop that is the subject of this report, one in a series of workshops made possible through a grant to the CFE from the National Science Foundation, is the starting point for that effort. The center's mission is to promote evidence-based policy analysis that both responds to current needs and anticipates future ones. This one-day workshop was designed as an initial step in exploring the research in cognition and developmental psychology that sheds light on children's capacity to learn mathematical and scientific ideas. The workshop brought experts together to discuss research on the ways children's cognitive capacities can serve as building blocks in the development of mathematical and scientific understanding. The workshop also focused on curricular and resource materials for mathematics and science found in early childhood education settings as a means to examine particular research-based assumptions that influence classroom practice.

The workshop was a collaborative effort in which the Mathematical Sciences Education Board and the Board on Science Education, both of which operate under the umbrella of CFE, ensured that the perspectives of both subjects were well represented. The committee that planned the workshop began with a charge that included these questions:

- What is the state of research into the basic cognitive building blocks in mathematics and science? What does this research base suggest about the development of conceptual underpinnings in these subject areas?
- Is there a body of research that addresses both conceptual development in these subject areas and environmental influences?
- How are these concepts now addressed across early childhood education settings in the United States?
- In what ways can the research about conceptual building blocks in early mathematics and science development be used to help minimize later achievement differences in these subject areas across racial and socioeconomic groups?

Researchers specializing in both mathematics and science were invited to provide an overview of the current state of the scholarship that addresses these questions. Experts in the development of science and mathematics curricula for very young children were invited to offer their perspectives and describe several working programs that promote science or mathematics learning. The committee that planned the workshop did not evaluate the effectiveness of these programs, but merely identified a variety of programs that it believed would provide the basis for a stimulating discussion of the topics it was charged to explore. This summary report of the discussions and presentations at the workshop is designed to frame the issues relevant to advancing research useful to the development of research-based curricula for mathematics and science for young children. All the invited experts were asked to provide their perspectives on a set of specific questions about research and practice (which are detailed in the next two sections).

A one-day workshop on such a complicated topic can provide only a starting point to guide policy makers, researchers, and education professionals. The sole purpose of this report is to describe the discussions that took place at that workshop. However, issues for further investigation are explored in two afterwords.

EARLY CHILDHOOD CARE AND EDUCATION

The nature of what is required to make sure that children begin kindergarten truly ready for school—and the importance of doing so—have become more widely understood in recent years. These developments have come during a period in which growing numbers of families have sought care of some sort for their young children. The percentage of women in the labor force grew from 33 percent in 1950 to 60 percent in 2000. In 2000, the percentage of mothers who work outside the home was at 73 percent, and it was 61 percent for mothers of children under 3 years of age (Committee for Economic Development, 2002, p. 7).

Thus, very young children need care as well as education, and the care available to families takes many forms. In 2001, 56.4 percent of children under the age of 5 were regularly attending a center-based early childhood care and education program (U.S. Department of Education, National Center for Education Statistics, 2004).[1] The learning that takes place in these centers varies widely. Although measuring the quality of early childhood education is complicated, a number of indicators suggest that many children, especially those living in poverty and with other risk factors, are "served in child care programs of such low quality that learning and development are not enhanced and may even be jeopardized" (National Research Council, 2001b, p. 8).

Even in centers that are making conscientious efforts to provide a rich learning environment, the nature of what they are providing seems to vary considerably. Each state regulates early childhood centers in its own way, while the federal regulatory structure focuses on health and safety; the regulations of many states have relatively little to say about the pedagogical content of programs (National Research Council, 2001b). As a consequence, many young children in

[1] Another way of considering how many children are in some kind of child care is through data collected by the Children's Foundation: it reports that in 2004 there were 117,284 licensed child care centers and 300,032 regulated family child care homes. The foundation estimates that many more home day care centers exist than are included in the data because they are not licensed. (see www.childrensfoundation.net [accessed 5/29/04]).

the United States may not be benefiting from the substantial body of knowledge that has accumulated about how they learn.

Few people would claim that research on young children's learning could by itself address all of the problems in the United States' approach to educating its youngest children. Nevertheless, research findings that have accumulated in recent decades provide a critical underpinning for improvements in policy and practice. Cognitive development in science and mathematics has received particular attention from scholars in recent years. The cognitive skills in mathematics and science displayed by young children are not only the roots of later literacy in those areas, they are also building blocks in the development of the capacity to comprehend complex relationships and reason about those relationships. Indeed, research has highlighted the importance of the link between early learning experiences and subsequent achievement (National Research Council and Institute of Medicine, 2000). Yet elementary school teachers observe a wide range in the children who come to them, in terms of their readiness for school in these critical areas. The deficits are most apparent in children with socioeconomic risk factors (National Research Council, 2001b).

A full discussion of the many factors that have stood in the way of the goal of providing all children with access to high-quality early education was beyond the scope of the workshop, which focused on the understanding of young children's capacities in mathematical and science thinking and on ways to better support learning in those two areas. Recent research has explored some facets of young children's growth in cognitive capacities that support later learning in mathematics and science, and the workshop began with an examination of some of the key results of that work.

2

Mathematical and Scientific Cognitive Development

The first half of the workshop focused on the understanding of young children's learning that has been gained through research. The presenters and discussants were guided by a set of questions, supplied in advance, that were designed to target the most fundamental developments in research on mathematics and science learning in very young children—and those with the greatest potential for informing instructional practice:

- How do children's reasoning capabilities—in mathematics or science—develop across the early childhood years?
- How do children's conceptual "building blocks"—in mathematics and science—develop across these years?
- In what ways do mathematical and scientific development in early childhood represent a distinct set of processes? An integrated process? And how do they relate to general development in early childhood?

Presentations by Rochel Gelman and Nora Newcombe addressed the questions in different ways; their presentations were followed by general discussion of the issues raised by the current state of the research.

LEARNING FROM CHILDREN—RESEARCH IN PRESCHOOL SETTINGS

Gelman began by describing research that she has conducted over many years with teachers and children at early childhood centers run by the University of California at Los Angeles (UCLA) and Rutgers University. Through a prekindergarten program called Preschool Pathways to Science (PrePS), Gelman and her colleagues have found ways to engage young children in complex scientific thinking using a coherent program that is sustained over extended periods of time. The program is designed as a collaboration among researchers and early childhood educators, and it is based on research indicating that young children are capable of building progressively on knowledge they gain in a particular domain (Gelman and Brenneman, 2004). The key finding from Gelman's work is that children may be capable of scientific thinking far more complex than most casual observers might expect, and than scholars such as Piaget had considered possible.

Gelman illustrated her remarks with examples of children's complex thinking drawn from her experiences with PrePS. In one example, the children were shown a set of pictures that included both depictions of real animals, though ones likely to be unfamiliar to the children (e.g., an echidna), and depictions of animal-like objects, including fanciful creatures and toys. Using a variety of different questioning strategies, Gelman and her team established that the children could successfully distinguish between the real and nonreal animals and between those that could or could not move on their own power, and they could even identify the features that helped them make these distinctions.

Gelman has drawn several conclusions from her work: perhaps the most important is that providing children with a mental structure to guide their learning is critical. Specifically, Gelman argues, young children have the capacity to build on mental structures, that is, to take new information or observations and link them to concepts they have already thought about. Children can be guided in the development of these cognitive building blocks—concepts such as the general characteristics of a living thing—so that they can develop ways of thinking scientifically or in the intellectual traditions of other domains.

Once a mental structure is in place, she argued, children are much more likely both to notice new data that fit with what they have already learned and to store data in such a way that they can build on it in the future. Conversely, when children lack a mental structure for organizing particular domains of knowledge, the significance of new data is not evident to them and they must either construct a new structure to accommodate it or fail to benefit from it. Gelman also argued that young children need to develop familiarity with the language of science as they are gaining conceptual knowledge. The two go hand in hand and support one another: if children begin learning the correct vocabulary for the scientific work they are doing (observing relevant features, measuring, experimenting, predicting, checking, recording, and the like), it will enhance their conceptual learning.

Throughout her remarks, Gelman stressed that the key to the successes she and her colleagues have had has been the opportunity to work over a long term. The goal for PrePS was, as she put it, to "move children onto relevant learning paths," and this is done by creating an "environment that is coherent and embedded throughout the year." Rather than inserting, for example, a week- or even month-long science unit into a curriculum filled with other activities, Gelman and her colleagues were able to incorporate opportunities for scientific thinking into the daily schedule, with tools, such as science notebooks in which the children recorded their observations using drawings, stamps, and other methods, that provide extended opportunities to follow up on patterns of change in the natural world.

The science that the children do throughout the year is designed to be interconnected and thus to encourage the children to develop conceptually connected knowledge, that is, to build successively on the mental structures they are developing. Thus, a unit on seeds can be used to develop a range of related scientific skills, such as prediction and observation, as the children explore what seeds do, how they can be recognized, and how they can be classified according to various characteristics. At the same time, the exploration of seeds can serve as a building block in a broader exploration of a question such as "how do living things grow and change?" What is learned about seeds and plants can then be compared, contrasted, and connected to findings about other living creatures that the children have studied.

Gelman acknowledged that the time spent on science in these centers came at the expense of time spent on other potentially beneficial enterprises, such as art, music, or other activities that relate to important goals for early learning, but she maintained that the goals they were able to achieve could not be duplicated in an abbreviated format. However, she argued, the lines between key preschool domains such as mathematics, literacy, and science need not be viewed rigidly, nor is the allocation of time a zero-sum game. Science can provide content for math and literacy activities, and math and literacy activities can be incorporated into science activities.

It has taken Gelman and her colleagues a number of years to develop their program and for the teachers to become fully competent at the kinds of practice it requires. Though Gelman believes the program could successfully be duplicated in other settings, she and her colleagues have had little opportunity to test the challenges this would present or to prepare the program to be scaled up so that it could be duplicated in large numbers without direct involvement from those who devised it. Research remains an integral component of the program: discoveries about children give rise to new research questions and paradigms, while collaboration between researchers and practitioners expands the thinking of both.

THEORETICAL EVOLUTION— NEW MODES OF EXPERIMENTATION

Nora Newcombe focused her remarks on the relationship between spatial and mathematical development. Her own research has focused on identifying emerging capabilities in babies and toddlers. She has found that the capacity for spatial perception is a particularly significant development for mathematics ability not only because of its obvious importance in geometry, but also because of its less obvious role in other kinds of mathematical thinking, such as doing word problems. Newcombe began by setting her research findings and her reactions to the workshop questions in the context of three distinct theoretical perspectives in the study of early learning—Piagetian, nativist, and neoconstructivist.

The work of Jean Piaget, whose work spanned the period from the 1930s to the 1950s, was considered revolutionary when first published and is still very influential in the education of early childhood teachers. Piaget believed that children are born with innate cognitive structures that are programmed to emerge in sequence as the child develops and that cognitive skills require relatively little environmental input in order to emerge (National Research Council and Institute of Medicine, 2000). Thus, as Newcombe explained, Piaget argued that particular cognitive building blocks, such as the ability to measure, will not be evident until their preordained time, at 5-6 years in the case of measurement. However, Newcombe pointed out, researchers since Piaget, including both Gelman and herself, have demonstrated that children can do many things, including measuring, much earlier than Piaget had believed was possible.

Researchers have found that Piaget's findings can generally be replicated if the questions are asked in the same way that he asked them, but that in many cases the findings look very different if the same question is asked in a different way. For example, Newcombe explained, Piaget assessed children's capacity to recognize how objects would look if viewed from a different vantage point by showing them photographs of a landscape with clearly identifiable features taken from different perspectives. He found that young children were unsuccessful at this task. However, when Newcombe and her colleagues presented the same task in a different way, by showing children a tableau of objects and asking "If you were sitting over there, what would be closest to you?" they found that children at the same ages Piaget tested were successful. In this context Newcombe noted that she finds the ubiquitous use of the term "developmentally appropriate" very troubling precisely because defining the skills that have developed by a particular age is so difficult.

Piaget's views were challenged by later researchers known as nativists, who argued, as Newcombe put it, that "there is both metric coding and number sensitivity as early as you can assess it." In other words, nativists believe that babies are born with significant capacities and that, with appropriate environmental cues, they can function cognitively in much more advanced ways than Piaget had believed.

The theoretical perspective that Newcombe referred to as neoconstructivism borrows from both of these earlier perspectives. In this view, which accords with Newcombe's, young children are seen as having "much stronger starting points" than Piaget had allowed, but as undergoing many subsequent developmental changes. According to this perspective, the effects of experience on young children's cognitive development are very important, and thus what happens in preschool is particularly critical.

Newcombe summarized the key points of difference among these three perspectives—Piaget and his followers, the nativists, and the neoconstructivists:

- the age at which competencies emerge;
- the degree of subsequent developmental change (i.e., how complete or developed the competencies are when they first emerge);
- the existence of initial modularity (i.e., the extent to which cognitive skills are differentiated at early ages); and
- the role played by environmental influences.

Newcombe's research has addressed the first two of these issues in specific ways. She and her colleagues have explored ways of assessing babies' and toddlers' thinking, for example, by asking them to find objects hidden in a sandbox or checking their reactions to changes in quantity and number. She has found that there are indeed stronger starting points than Piaget had believed. More specifically, she and other researchers have found that the spatial and quantitative domains seem to share a starting point, that is, to be two components of innate core knowledge, perhaps skills located in particular regions of the brain, and then differentiate at later stages of development (see Newcombe, 2002). Newcombe has also found evidence of developmental change. She noted significant increases in competence on the same task between, for example, 18- and 24-month-olds. She believes that while babies and toddlers are capable of more than Piaget claimed, they are also farther from adult levels of competence than nativists have claimed.

Newcombe noted that her claim about the common starting point for spatial and quantitative thinking remains controversial in the field and used that point to highlight the need for caution in presenting research findings of this kind to the public. As in the public health arena, she explained, new findings can be exciting and seem newsworthy. Practitioners may jump—or be encouraged—to try to incorporate them into their thinking and their practice, only to be disappointed when later findings seem to contradict them. When findings are presented as more certain than they really are, she noted, the result can be that over time the audience for such information becomes increasingly skeptical of new research.

IMPLICATIONS OF CURRENT RESEARCH

Much of the discussion that flowed from the two presentations centered around the question of what framework for understanding mathematical and scientific cognition in young children best fits the available research evidence. Kathleen Metz opened by noting that just as scientists and mathematicians generally operate in parallel spheres with relatively little interaction, cognitive scientists who study mathematics and science learning have tended to follow suit, with the result that there are two disjoint literatures on these topics. She asked whether there is a general theory of cognitive development that accounts for both domains, or whether children's development occurs in domain-specific ways, and, further, how progress in one domain might feed progress in the other.

Catherine E. Snow touched on the same point and pointed out that the presentations did not seem to have revealed "deep abstract parallel structures underlying mathematical and scientific development." Other participants identified some points of commonality, noting, for example, that cognitive skills such as sorting and sequencing are components of both domains. However, participants also noted that important differences between these two spheres remain unreconciled. In mathematics the content and skills are closely linked—that is, the capacity to enumerate objects is integrally related to understanding of numbers. In science, by contrast, the cognitive skills to be developed (e.g., observing, predicting, classifying) can be enumerated fairly easily, but the potential content domains in the context of which they might be learned (i.e., any aspect of the natural world that can be made accessible to a preschooler) are essentially limitless.

One participant challenged the notion of a preschool science curriculum by raising the question of whether children might actually be able to learn many science skills in nonscientific contexts, for example, by identifying the characteristics of different literary genres, taking notes, and presenting the results graphically. Nora Newcombe responded by suggesting that the goals for preschool- and elementary-level mathematics education are clearer, or at least more specific, than the goals for preschool- and elementary-level science, precisely because the potential domain of science is so broad.

The challenge of narrowing a science curricula provided one bridge to the discussion of preschool science curricula that dominated the afternoon. Several participants noted that while science and mathematics learning are undeniably important, they are only two on a long list of very important objectives for preschool education. In preschool contexts, it was argued, considerably more attention has been paid to the importance of literacy than to other domains, such as mathematics and science. Possible reasons for this focus were not brought out, but its pervasiveness was acknowledged.

Research on the development of cognitive skills related to mathematics and science has provided fascinating new pictures of what young children can do, but very little guidance for adults about how to use this information in caring for young children. Gregg Solomon highlighted this point by bringing to the discussion the perspective of one who makes decisions about which research to fund. Solomon's position allows him to observe several research literatures that all pertain to important questions about early learning but seldom benefit from one another. For example, he sees researchers who have developed curricula that seem both creative and effective and yet lack coherent, research-based rationales, and research into chemistry or physics learning that does not reflect current thinking from the cognitive science literature.

One important problem that results from the fact that so many researchers are not well versed in the developments in other, related, domains, Solomon explained, is that as key findings are summarized and passed on in new contexts, they are often distorted in the process. A single study that suggests an interesting possibility that calls for further investigation is often condensed and described in an oversimplified, exaggerated way. Teachers, the end users of much of this kind of information, are then provided with questionable versions of research findings, or research findings that do not correspond to one another or do not seem to be connected to a set of common ideas. As Newcombe had noted earlier, any oversimplification of research findings only fuels mistrust of future claims.

Noting that the discussion had ranged over a number of issues that call for further investigation, Sharon Lynn Kagan closed the morning discussion by asking the panelists to consider which of the many issues about which more research is needed are the most pressing and important. In response, Newcombe identified a basic research question. For her, the relationship between explicit and implicit knowledge—between action and cognition—is a fundamental issue about which significantly more needs to be known. In other words, while identifying the skills of which young children are capable and pinpointing the stages at which they develop particular skills is very useful, the next logical and necessary step is to understand how children apply these skills. With further insight into the uses children can and do make of the cognitive skills they seem to have at very young ages can come further insight into questions about school readiness and ways that it can be fostered for all racial and socioeconomic groups.

Gelman took a somewhat different tack. She described the additional research that would be needed to scale up her work with preschoolers, that is, to develop it to the point where it could be used effectively in any classroom. For her, however, this need relates to a larger question about the magnitude of the effects that children's communities, family backgrounds, and social circumstances have on their capacity to benefit from an enriched preschool environment. Her experiences with children from low- and middle-income families has led her to believe that many are being educated in cognitively deprived settings. She believes that because children's capacities have been consistently underestimated, the importance of enriched learning environments for young children has not been sufficiently recognized. At the same time, better understanding of how children's educational needs may vary according to the socioeconomic circumstances in which they live will be very useful in developing programs that meet all children's needs. Gelman hopes that preschool curricula can be developed that work despite inadequate teacher preparation, but she argued that improved preparation and ongoing development for teachers are critical. Research that provides more detailed understanding of children's capacities can support both of these goals.

As both of these responses to the question about research priorities make evident, the role of practice frequently found its way into the morning's discussion of research. While Gelman's research is conducted in a practice setting, Newcombe was also focused on the implications of her findings for the education of young children. The link between the two was the focus of the second half of the workshop.

3

Going from Knowledge to Practice

The second half of the workshop was designed to focus on the ways in which research is already influencing practice, as well as the ways in which it could be used to further improve the education of young children. The discussion quickly made clear that a model in which research is seen as the sole source of ideas that can be used to improve teaching does not capture the dynamic relationship between research and practice that already exists and that needs to be fostered. Most participants agreed that while research findings have much to offer practitioners, the reverse is also true and that the greatest wisdom is to be gotten from a situation in which research and practice can continually contribute to and gain from one another.

The presenters and discussants were guided by two broad questions:

- How is the research base on early mathematical and scientific cognitive development currently reflected in early childhood curricula and settings in the United States?
- What might be some specific implications of this research base for the improvement of early childhood education in science and mathematics?

Presenters Doug Clements, Lucia French, and Karen Worth drew on their experiences with early childhood programs in considering the role of research.

A UNION OF RESEARCH AND PRACTICE

Clements' presentation focused primarily on the second of the questions. He presented a model of how he believes research on young children's learning should proceed, without commenting directly on the ways in which research is currently influencing practice. He began by showing a set of slides of children of the same age demonstrating very different competencies, and asked: "What possible theory of curriculum in research is going to help us address [children at disparate levels] and help us figure out what best to do?" As he sees it, no theory, or even definition, of what a preschool curriculum should be is guiding current work or providing a framework for thinking and planning. What is needed is a true science of curriculum in mathematics, science, and other fields. By this he means a view of curriculum development that goes beyond the provision of practical feedback to those who develop curricula. He views the development of curricula as a form of inquiry that "provides reliable ways of dealing with experiences and achieving goals." Clements presented examples of the kinds of questions about curriculum he thought such a science of curriculum could help to address, with particular attention to its relationship to practice, policy, and theory; see Table 3-1.

Clements and his colleagues have developed an operating framework for thinking about curriculum research. Such research can begin with an *a priori* foundation, a broad philosophy of learning rooted in past research that yields a starting notion of the way children learn. Such research can also be organized around learning models, or, as he termed them, learning trajectories. These trajectories are pathways that children typically take through a series of levels or

TABLE 3-1 Questions That Can Be Answered with a Theory of Curriculum

	Practice	Policy	Theory
Effect	Is the curriculum effective in achieving learning goals? Is it credible relative to alternatives?	How much improvement or benefit does this curriculum offer? Are the goals set for this curriculum important?	Why is it effective? Is it credible relative to alternative theoretical approaches?
Conditions	When and where has it been used? Under what conditions has it been successful? Can it be easily used and successful in other settings?	What kinds of supports are needed for it to work in various contexts?	Why do different conditions increase or decrease its effectiveness? How and why do these strategies produce results others could not produce?

SOURCE: Douglas Clements

phases of understanding, and Clements demonstrated what he meant with illustrations of children responding in different ways to the same task. A curriculum based on this understanding is then designed to move children through a developmental progression, which in turn helps them achieve specific curricular goals.

Research designed to evaluate particular curricular approaches on the basis of this kind of theoretical underpinning, Clements argued, should then proceed through several steps. It should begin with small groups in which the phases of the learning trajectory can be closely evaluated to see whether the tasks and behaviors the curriculum elicits are as intended and whether the model needs to be modified for any reason. The next step would be to try out the model with whole classrooms, in which it is possible to evaluate teachers' and students' responses to it more thoroughly and identify both intended and unintended consequences.

The final stage would be to try out the model in multiple classrooms with the aim of assessing how it works when it is implemented in diverse settings by diverse teachers. It is at this stage that formative research methods, designed to yield ways of improving the program, give way to summative research, first on a small scale (e.g., four to ten classrooms) and then on a larger scale. Once the program has been improved, using the feedback obtained in the earlier phases, it would be time to use random assignment and other experimental methods to find out how robust the program is.

The key advantage of this approach, Clements explained, is that it "inoculates" researchers against "confirmation bias," the tendency to look for results that confirm their expectations. In other words, the early stages of the research provide low-risk opportunities to identify weaknesses, such as conditions in which the program does not succeed, unintended consequences, and so forth, and to make changes in response. The research process benefits from the feedback obtained from progressive stages of classroom experience with the model. Clements contrasted his model with what he regards as the more common "research-to-practice" approach to curriculum research in which, he argued, the flow of information is one way. When the flow is one way, there is little opportunity for practical experience to influence revision of theoretical assumptions that may be flawed.

At the same time, Clements noted, most of the curricula that are commercially available today are buttressed by market research rather than scholarship. Such curricula often include terminology from recent research in such a way as to seem to be in line with the most recent thinking without actually having incorporated substantive changes. He argued for the importance of a synthesis of curriculum development, practice, and research. Curriculum developers, he explained, can provide researchers with rich tasks, authentic settings, and theoretical problems that can inform their work. The experience of practitioners provides indispensable feedback about real-world effectiveness. Yet without research, developers and teachers may miss critical aspects of students' thinking and the particular features of a curriculum that engender learning.

PRESCHOOL SCIENCE AS A PROCESS

French approached the questions by describing the way science has been incorporated into the lives of preschoolers enrolled in a Head Start-based program called Science Start! This program, which is now operating in nearly 40 low- and middle-income schools in the Rochester, New York, area, uses science as the organizing core through which language and literacy and a variety of other preschool skills are taught (French, 2004).

The curriculum French and her colleagues, a team of researchers and practitioners, have devised, while not based in a particular theoretical perspective regarding the way young children learn science, is organized around the scientific processes as defined in the national science standards (National Research Council, 1996) and by the American Association for the Advancement of Science Benchmarks (American Association for the Advancement of Science, 1993), which include observing, comparing, classifying, measuring, sequencing, quantifying, representing data, interpreting representations, predicting, replicating, and reporting. The goal is to use children's innate curiosity about the natural world as the starting point for a range of activities that develop their language and other cognitive skills.

The children enrolled in the program participate in a daily cycle in which they begin in the morning by asking questions and reflecting on the topics presented by the teachers. They then plan a course of action and predict the results they think are likely. They execute their plans and observe what happens. They end the cycle by reporting on what they have observed and reflecting on their plans and their results. For French, part of the evidence of the program's success lies in the extent to which the children have been able, by the end of the school year, to take over responsibility for much of this scientific work. They have internalized the processes, she explained, and have learned ways of thinking scientifically.

At the same time, each of the science units incorporates, and is supported by, other kinds of activities designed to foster other kinds of cognitive growth. Books on related themes are read aloud, mathematics and social studies skills and content are brought in, and art and outdoor play activities with a link to the science theme are developed. The broad goals for the program include not only development of scientific thinking, but also of the capacity to use language to convey complex information and to do planning and problem solving. Development of other important preschool skills—such as self-control, working cooperatively in peer groups, and focusing attention—are also part of the program.

French showed participants a video of a group of children working through an activity that involved transforming carrots into baby food. They inspected some carrots, made predictions about ways of transforming them so a baby could eat them, and then ran them through a blender and ultimately fed them to a baby that was visiting the classroom. Some participants questioned French as to the nature of the science the children learned through this activity, and French's response was that the children demonstrated several of the processes mentioned above in the course of the activity—e.g., predicting what might happen and reflecting on the result.

French explained that in the course of the year a variety of material is presented; the original program began with 10-week units on measurement and mapping, color and light, matter, and the like. However, because the focus is on the scientific process, the program allows flexibility for the teachers to respond to the children's interests or to unexpected events outside or in the classroom that present a learning opportunity. While the teachers provide guidance in many ways, supplying suitable materials, asking questions designed to elicit scientific thinking, and so forth, the children can instigate projects or topics. Despite this flexibility, however, the program is designed to be coherent, both by allowing time for teachers and children to investigate each topic thoroughly and follow through on multistep activities, and also by using the daily instructional cycle to provide structure and consistency.

A key component of the Science Start! program has been professional development for the teachers. French's initial goal was that the teachers be prepared to use what she calls information-bearing language (in contrast with behavior-management language) as much as possible with the children, not just in response to questions they ask, and to focus on engaging their interests. This approach, French explained—teachers who consistently use scientific language and try to weave information into classroom conversations within the structure of the daily cycle—has worked to help the children develop sophisticated discourse patterns that reflect scientific thinking and also to show steady increases in vocabulary.

French and her colleagues have used several means of assessing the effectiveness of ScienceStart! They have distilled preschool-level benchmarks from those developed by the American Association for the Advancement of Science (1993) that they use as internal goals, such as "People can often learn about things around them just by observing those things carefully, but sometimes they can learn more by doing something to the things and noting what happens." They have also used what they call narrative assessments, storybooks in which a character asks questions of other characters; children being assessed are asked to respond before the story continues and observers can assess their mastery of concepts that have been addressed. The children have also been assessed using the Peabody Picture Vocabulary Test and have shown gains in vocabulary (French, 2004, pp. 7-10).

MAKING USE OF WHAT IS ALREADY KNOWN

Karen Worth began with a direct response to the first of the workshop questions, regarding the degree to which research is reflected in early childhood curricula and settings in the United States. Unfortunately, Worth has concluded, the answer is that the influence of research on science teaching and learning at the preschool level seems to have been minimal. Worth noted that there has been a tremendous amount of very exciting research in recent years, but that there is little parallel development in practice to point to, and called this disconnect "profound and disturbing." She also noted that many individual programs across the country are of very high quality and may be incorporating research findings, but that they are generally not replicated or widespread.

Far more common, Worth has observed, are settings in which little or nothing that is accomplished could truly be described as science. Centers might have a science table that is one among several activity centers children can choose, and it may have some science-related materials on it. Unfortunately, though, these centers are either seldom used, or used primarily for one-time activities that focus on arts-and-crafts projects that make use of materials or ideas with science content (e.g., leaves, birds nests, colored water, and absorbent paper) but yield a take-home product rather than mastery of a scientific concept or skill. Yet at the same time, Worth noted, other materials that are found in most preschool settings, such as blocks and building materials, cooking equipment, and sand and water tables and other outdoor equipment, could be used to help children develop science thinking but seldom are.

Even where more conscious emphasis is placed on science, she argued, the result is often activities that might last a week or two, in which a theme such as dinosaurs is explored, but which provide no connection to broader themes or continuous work on developing particular modes of scientific thinking. This approach is reflected in many of the science resource materials that are available for early childhood teachers. Worth argued that most of them are essentially fun activity books rather than curricula that reflect a research based notion of how children learn or well thought-through goals for their science learning.

In reference to the second workshop question, regarding ways in which research could more effectively be brought to bear on classroom practice in the future, Worth began by describing work that she has done through a National Science Foundation project developing materials for classrooms, teacher guides, and professional development guides. These materials have been constructed not only to incorporate sound research-based ideas about young children's learning, but also to get to teachers quickly and be truly usable and helpful. The goal for this project was to take the significant body of sound research findings that are already available and find ways to bring it into the classroom without waiting for further refinements.

In developing these curricula, Worth and her colleagues decided to begin with materials they could safely assume would be in most preschool classrooms.

Thus, the first three teacher guides they developed focused on blocks and building, water, and the immediate outside environment. While the guides are not prescriptive, Worth explained, they provide a structure that leads from open experimentation to more focused exploration and guides teachers regarding the different kinds of roles they can play in the process to foster children's learning. Worth closed her remarks by providing summaries of the characteristics of an effective science program and of the roles of an effective teacher (see Boxes 3-1 and 3-2). She used these to illustrate what is for her perhaps the most important dimension in the enterprise, the preparation of teachers.

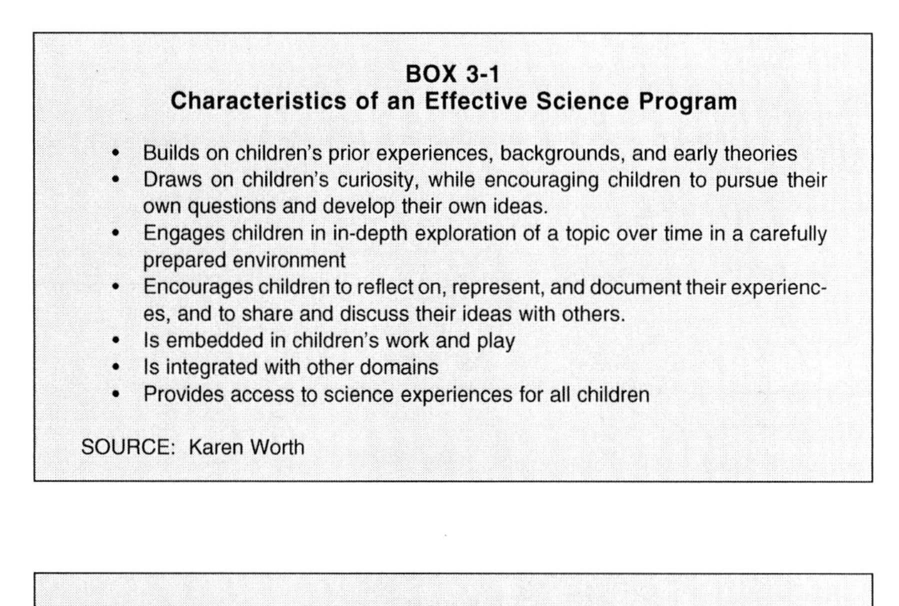

BOX 3-1
Characteristics of an Effective Science Program

- Builds on children's prior experiences, backgrounds, and early theories
- Draws on children's curiosity, while encouraging children to pursue their own questions and develop their own ideas.
- Engages children in in-depth exploration of a topic over time in a carefully prepared environment
- Encourages children to reflect on, represent, and document their experiences, and to share and discuss their ideas with others.
- Is embedded in children's work and play
- Is integrated with other domains
- Provides access to science experiences for all children

SOURCE: Karen Worth

BOX 3-2
Roles of an Effective Teacher

- Creates a physical, social, and emotional environment that supports inquiry
- Observes children and acts on those observations
- Acknowledges children's work
- Extends children's experiences, which are based in their work
- Leads activities with children that extend their thinking
- Deepens children's understanding through discussion, questions, representation, and documentation

SOURCE: Karen Worth

For Worth, the science content of preschool education is crucial. While she agreed that there is not a finite number of topics that must be covered, for her it is nevertheless very important that young children be working on topics and concepts that are fundamental to science, not just random topics that seem interesting. Thus, the questions of how much knowledge, what kind of knowledge, and what kind of preparation and support teachers need assume critical importance. Worth argued that teachers need to know far more science than they currently do; "They have to have inquired before they can help children inquire. They have to know where children's inquiries might go conceptually in a science field in order to both understand and follow children."

4

Learning Environments and Curriculum

The presentations stimulated discussion about a number of topics, and implications for research, practice, and policy were suggested throughout. Much of the discussion clustered around three themes that closely matched those posed by the workshop planning committee. The relationship between cultural and socioeconomic factors and cognitive development in mathematics and science was clearly important to many participants. Participants also saw the question of how a preschool curriculum should be defined and what goals it should serve as very important. Finally, the ways in which research on children's developing cognitive capacities can provide near-term benefits to young children in terms of improved curricular materials was a recurring theme.

CULTURAL AND SOCIOECONOMIC INFLUENCES ON DEVELOPMENT

The issue of cultural biases that may be embedded in some of the expectations people have of the way young children should learn and behave came up in a number of contexts. Barbara Bowman raised the question in the context of the classroom videotape shown by Lucia French, in which several of the children were distracted from the planned activity and doing other things, while others were attending closely and responding to the teacher's cues. Bowman's query was about identifying the boundary between the essential components of cognition and the expectations that grow out of particular cultural contexts. Bowman suggested that very different approaches to pedagogy in other countries, such as

Iran or China, in which she believes that much more rigid behavioral structures are imposed on very young children, seem to yield not only very successful adult scientists, but also students who can flourish in U.S. colleges. She raised the question of how one might identify the critical elements of learning behavior and distinguish them from cultural habits.

In response, several participants acknowledged that current cognitive research may not make it possible to identify a precise boundary between components of cognition common to all and intellectual traditions that develop in particular cultures, but cautioned that this level of precision may be beside the point. Children need to learn to operate within the cultures of science and mathematics as they are in the cultures in which they live. The cognitive and cultural components of the expectations adults have may be intertwined, but teaching is also embedded in a cultural context, and the task at hand is to find the best ways to use teaching to help children develop the kinds of thinking they will need as they grow to adulthood. Karen Worth noted that whether inquiry is a purely intellectual notion or a partly cultural one, it is clearly recognized as an integral aspect of science, as evidenced in the science standards and elsewhere, and its intrinsic value is not in question.

However, Bowman argued that not all children in the United States are experiencing the mainstream cultural context and that these differences can have effects that are observable at very young ages. Prentice Starkey pointed out that differences that match up with socioeconomic status are evident in children as young as 3, and he added that while Japanese and Chinese 4-year-olds are approximately 1 year ahead of middle-class American children, those middle-class children are about 1 year ahead of low-income children in the United States. He reiterated the importance of examining more closely the influence of children's learning environments on their developing mathematics and science knowledge.

Other differences among children could interact with their science and mathematics learning as well, in ways that are not well understood. Participants pointed out that gender differences, as well as ability differences and differences in learning style or intellectual approach, may well affect the ways children respond to teaching and the ways they learn, but these issues in preschoolers have not yet been much studied.

Without questioning the importance of that goal, however, Nora Newcombe pointed out the significant methodological and practical challenges to that kind of research. She noted that such links are much easier to track in the context of language development because one needs only a fairly brief tape of parents' conversation that can be coded for syntactic complexity and other features to get a measure of a child's environment. In the case of mathematics and science, however, the kinds of actions and conversation from parents that can enhance development would not generally occur frequently enough for a random sample of interaction to capture them. Moreover, the kinds of parental inputs that are beneficial can vary widely and may not be as readily identified and described or as readily captured on audiotape. Her point was not that such research should not be attempted but that because of its expense it may not be the source of much near-term benefit.

In contrast, Doug Clements pointed out that cultural differences can be taken into account in other ways. In his model for developing curricula, for example, the process of trying things out in different kinds of classrooms, in increasing numbers at each stage, allows researchers and developers to adapt a program so that it can be used successfully in very different settings without the underpinning of refined research such as that described by Newcombe.

Another facet of this conversation related to more structural issues about how preschool education is delivered. Preschool has not been widely seen as a high priority in the United States (though that is beginning to change) and is consequently perennially underfunded. Salaries and benefits for preschool and early childhood teachers are at the very lowest levels on the spectrum for teachers, and indeed for U.S. workers; consequently the turnover rate is very high—43 percent, as Sharon Lynn Kagan noted. Job requirements for teachers in licensed centers are low, and a significant percentage of children are likely served in unlicensed settings that are not regulated at all. The children most likely to be found in the least beneficial settings are those who already face such disadvantages as low family income and low levels of parental education. While efforts are being made in a number of states to improve both the training and ongoing development of preschool educators and the professional benefits available to them, the current state of affairs nevertheless raises questions about what can reasonably be expected of the corps of teachers who are currently teaching the majority of young children. These points provided one link to the discussion about what a curriculum for preschool should be expected to accomplish.

WHAT IS A PRESCHOOL CURRICULUM?

Underlying the discussion of preschool curricula was recognition that defining what is meant by that term is not straightforward. Participants recognized that it can serve as shorthand for notions of what content should be presented, how content is presented, who is responsible for determining the details of what is presented, and the like. The discussion did not resolve these potentially conflicting ideas about what curriculum means in a preschool context but addressed them from a variety of angles.

A starting question about goals for a preschool curriculum is just how prescriptive it should be. One view is based on the current reality that the teaching force at this level is generally characterized by inadequate preparation and offered inadequate ongoing professional development and that these teachers generally have few years of experience because of high turnover rates. Given this reality, it may be logical to offer them comprehensive, detailed curricula that can help them succeed even without having had strong preparation and experience.

Participants took this point seriously, but noted at the same time that big questions remain not only about what should be in such a prescriptive curriculum, but also about who should be responsible for developing it, ensuring its quality, and overseeing its implementation. Moreover, some people argued that teachers cannot really succeed if they do not fully grasp the underlying educational intent of the program they are instituting, so that professional development for teachers deserves as much consideration as student learning.

At present, participants noted, many different kinds of curricula are in use, and some efforts have been made to categorize them to get a sense of the balance that currently exists among different approaches. At the same time, however, others cautioned that what many people refer to as a curricular approach is really a pedagogical style. Teachers and centers that use the Reggio Emilia or Montessori approach, for example, are subscribing to theories of the way children should be taught, rather than signing on to teach children particular content or even particular academic skills. The overlap between the concepts of curriculum and pedagogical approach was explicitly acknowledged, along with the recognition that each has a role to play in a consideration of the content and teaching methods that are effective in early learning settings.

Some participants spoke up for understanding a preschool curriculum in much the same way curricula for older children are viewed, as a specification of concepts to be taught. At the same time, Catherine E. Snow, for example, argued that even a program such as High/Scope, which is intended as a curriculum, stops short of the level of specificity that she would describe as a curriculum.

For Karen Worth the issue was one of depth. A curriculum, she argued, should not just list "the life cycle," for example, as a topic to be covered, but specify what children should come to understand about it. Noting that the life cycle is also a graduate-level topic, she explained that simply observing the life cycle of a single animal would not yield the understanding that she would consider adequate for preschoolers. A curriculum should explicitly direct that the children be guided in exploring the life cycles of different plant and animal species and helped to link these observations to broad biological concepts that have been specified. She argued, further, that there should be, if not a finite list of scientific topics that must be covered in the preschool years, a clearly defined set of concepts from which preschool curricula should draw.

Another approach, Nora Newcombe pointed out, would be to use the objectives for elementary school mathematics and science to guide the development of a preschool curriculum. While she expressed hesitation about how readily this could be done, she argued that it is the long-term goals for development in mathematics and science that provide the best guide to what preschoolers should be doing.

Sharon Lynn Kagan raised the related issues of the pros and cons of having formal standards that could guide the development of individual curricula, as well as the question of when and how preschool children's development in mathematics and science should be assessed. Several participants were quick to point out that the kind of assessment that would be most useful with young children is the formative kind that allows teachers to see what children have learned and tailor their practice to improve learning.

Questions about assessment relate directly to policy questions about the ways in which early childhood education is regulated. As has been noted, the regulatory structure at this level is significantly less thorough than that which governs K-12 education. One implication of that fact is that it is not obvious who has the responsibility for devising curricula, what qualifications curriculum developers ought to have, or which institutions ought to play a role in such a process. More fundamentally, participants pointed out that many, many children are not now benefiting from any curriculum or particular pedagogical approach at all, so the baseline for improvement is, for those children, exceedingly low. While no one questioned the absolute benefits of identifying ambitious goals for mathematics and science education in the early childhood context, the importance of addressing the most urgent needs—that is, of making use of what is already known to ameliorate the inadequacies of the preschool settings in which many children are enrolled, immediately—was articulated many of times.

MAKING THE MOST OF RESEARCH

The urgency of some of the problems with early childhood education was at the root of many participants' comments about the role research can and should play. First, it was clear from both presentations and discussion that a significant body of sound research is already available and that much of this research has not been adequately mined for contributions to practice. However, participants also noted some problems. As Gregg Solomon and others pointed out, when new research that has not yet been adequately vetted in its professional context makes its way prematurely into the public eye, it can have a harmful rather than a helpful effect. At the same time, the existence of many inconsistencies both within and among fields, in terms of both findings and their implications, means that many research results are not yet useful to practitioners, curriculum developers, and others.

Second, there is a tendency, which probably exists in virtually all scholarly fields, for researchers to pinpoint targets that are so narrow that the results have little apparent application. Kathleen Metz cited as an example the large body of research on the errors children make in doing subtraction. Given that this research thread does not address strategies for helping them avoid errors, or other related questions, its benefit to teachers is not evident. While it may offer theoretical insights that provide benefits down the road, Metz's point was that such work may not be the highest priority.

Although many participants seemed to agree on the importance of research models in which both theoretical research goals and methods and the practical experience gained in the classroom have influence, a caveat was raised. Although the value of practical knowledge seems clear, it is important to remember that it does not offer the same possibility of reliability that formal research does. In general, there are only informal ways to try to replicate practice to confirm the conclusions it seems to yield, and there is an ever present danger that anecdotal experience might be confused with confirmed results. Nevertheless, maintaining tight connections to classroom experience seems to offer researchers an important way of guarding against a variety of pitfalls.

Reflecting on the day's discussion, participants agreed that a clear challenge is to determine how the available research fits together and to identify findings that are sufficiently robust to be trustworthy guides for action, as well as developed at a level of detail that makes them meaningful at a practical level. A number of research questions and goals were identified throughout the day as having particular merit in the context of what many participants regarded as urgent problems with the current state of preschool education, and the report closes with these.

- What are young children (3- and 4-year-olds) capable of learning? What is the floor (or ceiling) of their competence?
- What is there to be learned from international colleagues and practical experience in other countries?
- What are the learning trajectories in the domains of mathematics and science?
- What role does the integration of knowledge across mathematics and science play in children's learning trajectories?
- What principles should guide decisions regarding content for preschool curricula?
- How can children in different environments best be supported in learning mathematics and science?

Afterword: Child Care and Preschool Education

Catherine E. Snow

Currently, research and policy related to young children can be segmented into two major strands, each driven by a particular set of questions relevant to policy, learning, and economics. One strand is directed to issues of availability of and access to care and generates such questions as: What child care facilities must be provided to enable mothers to work? How can child care be financed so it is available to low-income families? How can child care be organized to meet the needs of parents working two jobs or swing shifts? What should the licensing requirements for child care centers be? In what sized groups should preschool-aged children spend their days?

The second strand is focused on issues of education—and, emblematically, the term *preschool* is then often substituted for *child care*, though the same settings are being discussed. Questions related to this strand include: What kinds of qualifications should the adults in preschool settings have? What kindergarten-readiness skills should preschools be responsible for producing? What curricula should preschools adopt? How much should those curricula be adult designed or child selected? How much should those curricula focus on content and how much on process?

Unfortunately, discussions related to the first strand, including consideration of financing, minimal licensing standards, and the schedules for care, tend to surround the child care settings serving the poorest families—families leaving welfare, families in which parents are working at low-income jobs, and families that have few resources of time, money, or knowledge to use in preparing their children for school. Discussions related to the second strand including attention to educational goals and standards, tend to be considered for the settings in which children from middle-income families spend their preschool years. These middle-income parents are generally less limited by cost and can select preschools on the basis of pedagogical approach, teacher qualifications, and curricular richness, rather than needing to focus on price and convenience.

This split between care and education, between logistical and educational issues, between policies for child safety and those for child development is one we can only deplore. Experience in child care, preschool, or prekindergarten has been shown, in an analysis of the data from the Early Childhood Longitudinal Kindergarten Study, to relate to later child outcomes in both literacy and math (Magnuson, Meyers, Ruhm, and Waldvogel, 2004). That same study showed that children from low-income families were less likely than others to have education experiences during their preschool years—though children whose parents had the lowest educational levels showed the greatest gains as a result of such experiences.

Previous reports of the National Research Council (NRC) have emphasized the importance of excellent preschool environments in promoting children's opportunities to benefit from kindergarten and subsequent progress in school. *Preventing Reading Difficulties in Young Children* (1998) emphasized the opportunities for language and early literacy development available in good preschool settings. *Eager to Learn: Educating Our Preschoolers* (2001b) proposed eliminating the rhetorical distinction between care and education and noted the availability (but limited distribution) of excellent preschool curricular materials and designs. *From Neurons to Neighborhoods: The Science of Early Childhood Development* (2000) emphasized the wide array of factors that influence development and argued convincingly that a scientific basis does exist for making decisions about caring for and educating young children.

Most of the research-based work on optimal design of preschool experiences has focused on language and literacy as the outcomes of interest. Indeed, there is evidence that literacy skills are more subject to environmental influences than are math skills (Jordan, Huttenlocher, and Levine, 1992). But social class differences in mathematics and science achievement are not negligible. Moreover, young children in particular acquire knowledge about literacy, mathematics, and science in much the same way—through conversations with adults and by being read to from information-rich books. In other words, rich language interactions are a key source of all these forms of learning. The agenda to guide future research on early learning within mathematics and science, following on the path of literacy and, perhaps, in concert with literacy, needs to be thoughtfully built through the kinds of conversations that occurred during this one-day NRC event.

The presentations at the workshop, summarized in this volume, reflect how much we can learn from developmental researchers who focus on children's accomplishments in the preschool years. But children can only accomplish so much on their own. Adults worried about the availability and financing of child care need to work with adults worried about education to convert care settings for preschoolers into rich opportunities for them to talk and learn about the worlds of science and math.

Afterword: Next Steps

Jean Moon and Heidi Schweingruber

Without a doubt there is a growing recognition of the importance of supporting the development of mathematical and scientific knowledge and skills in young children. As the workshop discussions and research show, a strong case can be made that young children are capable of surprisingly sophisticated thinking. Moreover, there is some evidence that gaps in capacities in mathematics and science can be linked to such environmental factors as economic disadvantage and may appear early in a child's development (Coley, 2002; Lee and Burkham, 2002; Starkey and Klein, 1992; Starkey, Klein and Wakeley, 2004). This evidence argues for attention to the research about how development in these specific domains unfolds, how capacities in different domains may be related, and how development of mathematical and scientific capacities can best be supported.

The interest and enthusiasm expressed by workshop participants indicate that both researchers and practitioners see a need for greater attention to research on mathematics and science in early childhood. The nineteenth volume of the *Early Childhood Research Quarterly* devoted to research on mathematics and science, to which many workshop participants contributed, offers further evidence of a strong commitment in the early childhood research community to advance work in this area. Yet most of the attention at the policy level to date has focused on literacy—for example, in the administration's policy initiative Good Start, Grow Smart, and in federally funded programs to support early childhood education, such as Early Reading First. Because the focus on literacy may lessen the amount of time educators have available for mathematics and science activities, it is particularly important to provide them with research-based information and strategies that will help them to make the best use of the time they can spend on mathematics and science.

As Nora Newcombe and other presenters pointed out, the last several decades of developmental research have resulted in the recognition that young children and even infants are capable of more sophisticated thinking and learning than was once assumed. Modern research in developmental psychology describes unexpected competencies in young children and calls into question models of development based on Piaget, which suggested that children were unable to carry out sophisticated cognitive tasks, such as perspective taking or measuring (Gelman and Brenneman, 2004; Newcombe, 2002; National Research Council and Institute of Medicine, 2000). As noted in the National Research Council report *Eager to Learn*:

> More recent research has led many to reinterpret the stage theorists' views; there is strong evidence that children, when they have accumulated substantial knowledge, have the ability to abstract well beyond what is ordinarily observed. Indeed, the striking feature of modern research is that it describes unexpected competencies in young children, key features of which appear to be universal. These data focus attention on the child's exposure to learning opportunities, calling into question simplistic conceptualizations of developmentally appropriate practice that do not recognize the newly understood competencies of very young children, and they highlight the importance of individual differences in children, their past experiences, and their present contexts (2001b, p. 5).

With recognition of these early competencies has come a reassessment of what children are capable of learning in the early years and how adults can best support this learning. For example, Rochel Gelman's discussion of the Preschool Pathways in Science program suggests that specific instruction in biology supported the development of children's ability to identify and sort animals and plants into appropriate categories and describe the features they used to carry out the sorting. As Gelman's example illustrates, the implications of advances in developmental research for mathematics and science learning in early childhood settings are profound. Working within a Piagetian framework, many early childhood educators were led to conclude that pushing children to undertake complex tasks in mathematic and science was fruitless. Children simply were not ready to think in scientific and mathematical ways. Evidence of early competence, especially where the development of such competence can be enhanced through instructional interventions, turns this kind of assumption on its head.

Some researchers point out, however, that simply demonstrating early competence does not provide a picture of the developmental processes involved in attaining such competency, nor the ways in which early competency serves as a foundation for later developments (Haith and Benson, 1998; Keil, 1998 cited in Kuhn, 2000; Ginsburg and Golbeck, 2004). Newcombe's presentation offered an example in the spatial and quantitative domains of how studies can be drawn together to reveal how and when early competencies first emerge, the limits of competence, and how competence changes with development. This outline of a developmental trajectory is potentially of greater interest to practitioners than the simple knowledge that children show competency early in their development. Bringing together the existing work in developmental psychology with research focused more specifically in mathematics and science education may begin to elucidate these kinds of developmental trajectories and clarify the most fruitful directions for future research.

Another newly emerging perspective on cognitive development also has profound implications for mathematics and science in early childhood education. Domain-specific theories of cognitive development posit that there are innate, domain-specific mental structures that underpin and guide learning in particular knowledge areas, such as biology or physics. This perspective is in contrast to traditional developmental theories of learning, such as those proposed by Piaget or Vygotsky, which describe general cognitive processes that operate similarly regardless of the content of cognition (Gelman and Brenneman, 2004; Newcombe, 2002). Some researchers go further to suggest that children actually develop naïve theories in a particular domain—for example, an understanding of the psychology of other people—and that developmental changes in children's knowledge rest in part on gathering evidence and revising these theories (Wellman and Gelman, 1998).

A domain-specific view raises critical questions, touched on by workshop presenters, about how learning unfolds in mathematics and science. For example: To what extent do learning in mathematics and learning in science unfold along separate and disconnected pathways? To what extent and how does learning in one domain inform the other? Are there some foundational competencies that underlie or support development in both mathematics and science?

One such foundational competency might be spatial reasoning. As noted by Newcombe (2002), even infants as young as 5 months show sensitivity to spatial cues when searching for hidden objects. These early spatial abilities might support such later mathematical concepts in geometry as transformations and symmetry, or locations, directions, and coordinates, both of which are suggested as among the key ideas for pre-K through grade 2 (Clements and Conference Working Group, 2004). Similarly, spatial reasoning might underlie the development of more formal concepts in physics (Gelman and Brenneman, 2004). Other cognitive abilities that might support both mathematics and science learning include categorization, symbolic reasoning, and causal reasoning.

Unfortunately, these advances in understanding of children's thinking do not seem to be shaping practice and policy in early childhood. Indeed, the workshop presenters and participants bemoaned the tremendous gaps between what is known from developmental research and the usual content of curricula and the nature of practice in early childhood settings. Furthermore, when applied research is carried out, it is often not guided by theoretical frameworks and does not draw on research on cognitive development, as Clements and Worth pointed out.

The lack of connection between current research and practice in this field is not unfamiliar to researchers and practitioners. The NRC reports *Eager to Learn* (National Research Council, 2001b) and *From Neurons to Neighborhoods* (National Research Council and Institute of Medicine, 2000) both emphasize the importance of better aligning research and work on translating that research into practice, taking into account the complexities of educational settings. *From Neurons to Neighborhoods* concludes that "as the rapidly evolving science of early child development continues to grow, its complexity will increase and the distance between the working knowledge of service providers and the cutting edge of the science will be staggering. The professional challenges that this raises for the early childhood field are formidable" (p. 42).

The key question then is how evidence from the most recent research in cognitive development can find its way into the worlds of policy and practice. The influence of research on the development of literacy skills demonstrates that a strong research base can influence policy and practice. The research base in mathematics and science is weaker than that in literacy, with less developed basic and applied research and fewer longitudinal studies (especially in science). In order to build from and strengthen this existing research base substantial work must be done to draw together the disparate strands into a coherent framework to identify both what is known and where the most promising future lines of research may lie.

The danger, of course, is to want to rush determinedly toward knitting together research and practice too early, before there is a deeper understanding of where the productive research intersections are and how those intersections may be useful to early childhood educators and curriculum developers. This rush to application with tentative findings was cautioned against by several workshop participants. The thrust of discussions suggested instead that the gap between research and practice cannot be closed until existing lines of research concerning children's learning of mathematical and scientific ideas are evaluated systematically and integrated into a more coherent picture of development. Only then can the areas in which further research is needed and those where the research evidence is sufficiently robust to inform practice be identified. In sum, a synthesis study that pulls together the applicable lines of research from developmental psychology, cognitive science, and applied research in early childhood settings to clarify what is known about very young children's ability to engage in mathematics and science is a logical next step in advancing both research and practice in these domains.

References

American Association for the Advancement of Science. (1993). *Project 2061 benchmarks for science literacy.* New York: Oxford University Press.

Clements, D., and Conference Working Group. (2004). Part one: Major themes and recommendations. In D.H. Clements, J. Sarama, and A.-M. DiBiase (Eds.), *Engaging young children in mathematics education* (pp. 1-72). Mahwah, NJ: Lawrence Erlbaum Associates.

Coley, R. (2002). *An uneven start: Indicators of inequality in school readiness.* Princeton, NJ: Educational Testing Service.

Committee for Economic Development. (2002). *Preschool for all: Investing in a productive and just society.* Washington, DC: Author.

French, L. (2004). Science as the center of a coherent, integrated, early childhood curriculum. *Early Childhood Research Quarterly, 19*(1), 138-149.

Gelman, R., and Brenneman, K. (2004). Science learning pathways for young children. *Early Childhood Research Quarterly, 19*(1), 150-158.

Ginsburg, H.P., and Golbeck, S.L. (2004). Thoughts on the future of research on mathematics and science learning and education. *Early Childhood Research Quarterly, 19*(1), 190-200.

Haith, M. M., and Benson, J.B. (1998). Infant cognition. In W. Damon (Series Ed.) and D. Kuhn and R. Siegler (Vol. Eds.), *Handbook of child psychology: Vol. 2, Cognition, language and perception* (5th ed.). New York: Wiley.

Jordan, N.C., Huttenlocher, J., and Levine, S.C. (1992). Differential calculation abilities in young children from middle- and low-income families. *Developmental Psychology, 28,* 644-653.

Kuhn, D. (2000). Developmental origins of scientific thinking. *Journal of Cognition and Development, 1,* 113-129.

Lee, V., and Burkham, D. (2002). *Inequality at the starting gate: Social background differences in achievement as children begin school.* Washington, DC: Economic Policy Institute.

Magnuson, K.A., Meyers, M.K., Ruhm, C.J., and Waldfogel, J. (Spring 2004). Inequality in preschool education and school readiness. *American Educational Research Journal, 41*(1), 115-157.

National Research Council. (1996). *National science education standards.* National Committee on Science Education Standards and Assessment. Center for Science, Mathematics, and Engineering Education. Washington, DC: National Academy Press.

National Research Council. (1998). *Preventing reading difficulties in young children.* C.E. Snow, M.S. Burns, and P. Griffin (Eds.). Committee on the Prevention of Reading Difficulties in Young Children. Commission on Behavioral and Social Sciences and Education. Washington, DC: National Academy Press.

National Research Council. (2001a). *Adding it up: Helping children learn mathematics.* Mathematics Learning Study Committee, J. Kilpatrick, J. Swafford, and B. Findell (Eds.). Center for Education, Division of Behavioral and Social Sciences and Education. Washington DC: National Academy Press.

National Research Council (2001b). *Eager to learn: Educating our preschoolers.* Committee on Early Childhood Pedagogy. B.T. Bowman, M.S. Donovan, and M.S. Burns (Eds.). Commission on Behavioral and Social Sciences and Education. Washington, DC: National Academy Press.

National Research Council and Institute of Medicine. (2000). *From neurons to neighborhoods: The science of early childhood development.* Committee on Integrating the Science of Early Childhood Development, J.P. Shonkoff and D.A. Phillips (Eds.). Board on Children, Youth, and Families, Commission on Behavioral and Social Sciences and Education. Washington, DC: National Academy Press.

Newcombe, N. (2002). The nativist-empiricist controversy in the context of recent research on spatial and quantitative development. *Psychological Science, 13*(5), 395-401.

Starkey, P. and Klein, A. (1992). Economic and cultural influence on early mathematical development. In F.L. Parker, R. Robinson, S. Sombrano, C. Piotrowski, J.Hagen, S. Randolph, and A. Baker (Eds.), *New directions in child and family research: Shaping Head Start in the 90's* (pp. 4-40). New York: National Council of Jewish Women.

Starkey, P., Klein, A., and Wakeley, A. (2004). Enhancing young children's mathematical knowledge through a pre-kindergarten mathematics intervention. *Early Childhood Research Quarterly, 19*(1), 99-120.

U.S. Department of Education, National Center for Education Statistics. (2004). *The condition of education 2004.* (NCES–077). Washington, DC: U.S. Government Printing Office.

Wellman, H. and Gelman, S. (1998). Knowledge acquisition in foundational domains. In W. Damon (Series Ed.) and D. Kuhn and R. Siegler (Vol. Eds.), *Handbook of child psychology: Vol. 2, Cognition, language and perception* (5th ed., pp. 523-574). New York: Wiley.

Appendix A

Workshop Agenda

Workshop on
Mathematical and Scientific Development in Early Childhood

National Research Council
The Keck Center, Rm. 201
500 Fifth Street, NW, Washington, DC 20001

AGENDA
Monday, March 22, 2004

NOTICE: This meeting is being audiotaped. Neither these tapes nor any transcripts of these tapes may be made available to the public without the prior written approval of the institution through the NRC Executive Office. A photo ID is required to enter The National Academies buildings.

8:30 a.m. Continental Breakfast

8:45 a.m. Welcome and Introduction to the Workshop
Carole Lacampagne, Director,
Mathematical Sciences Education Board
Jean Moon, Director, Board on Science Education
Catherine E. Snow (Chair), Harvard University

9:00 a.m. Panel I

Mathematical and Scientific Cognitive Development in Early Childhood

Jean Moon, National Research Council–Panel Moderator

Overview of Panel

Kathleen Metz, University of California, Berkeley

Presentations

Rochel Gelman, Rutgers University

Nora Newcombe, Temple University

10:00 a.m. Initial Response to Panel

Catherine E. Snow, Harvard University

Kathleen Metz, University of California, Berkeley

10:30 a.m. Break

10:45 a.m. Audience Discussion

11:30 a.m. Panel I Summary and Reflections

Gregg Solomon, National Science Foundation

11:45 a.m. Lunch

1:00 p.m. Panel II

Going from Knowledge to Practice

Carole Lacampagne, National Research Council–Panel Moderator

Overview of Panel

Sharon Kagan, Columbia University

Presentations by Panel Members

Doug Clements, State University of New York, Buffalo

Lucia French, University of Rochester

Karen Worth, Education Development Center, Newton, MA

2:00 p.m. Initial Response to Panel

Barbara Bowman, Erikson Institute, Chicago, IL

Sharon Kagan, Columbia University

2:30 p.m.	Break
2:45 p.m.	Audience Discussion
3:30 p.m.	Panel II Summary and Reflections *Sharon Kagan, Columbia University*
3:45 p.m.	Final Wrap-up *Catherine E. Snow (Chair), Harvard University*
4:45 p.m.	Meeting Adjourns

Appendix B

Workshop Participants

PRESENTERS

Doug Clements, State University of New York, Buffalo
Lucia French, Warner School of Education, University of Rochester
Rochel Gelman, Rutgers Center for Cognitive Science, Rutgers University
Nora S. Newcombe, Department of Psychology, Temple University
Gregg Solomon, Division of Elementary, Secondary, and Informal Education, National Science Foundation
Karen Worth, Education Development Center, Newton, MA

OTHER PARTICIPANTS

Daniel B. Berch, National Institute of Child Health and Human Development, National Institutes of Health
Toni Bickart, Teaching Strategies, Inc., Washington, DC
Jodi Jacobson Chernoff, Education Statistics Services Institute, Washington, DC
Diane Trister Dodge, Teaching Strategies, Inc., Washington, DC
Suzanne Donovan, National Research Council
Caroline Ebanks, Institute of Education Sciences, U.S. Department of Education
Patricia Freitag, National Science Foundation
Ruth Friedman, House Committee on Education and the Workforce, U.S. Congress

Charles Gallistel, Center for Cognitive Science, Rutgers University
Charles Hohmann, High/Scope Educational Research Foundation, Ypsilanti, MI
Mary Hohmann, High/Scope Educational Research Foundation, Ypsilanti, MI
Ivelisse Martinez-Beck, Child Care Bureau, Washington, DC
Christine Massey, Pre-College Research and Education, University of Pennsylvania
Monica Neagoy, Division of Elementary, Secondary, and Informal Education, National Science Foundation
Jennifer Park-Jadotte, Teaching Strategies, Inc., Washington, DC